It starts from their early beginnings in rough chronology through to the present day.

The book includes sections of multiple-choice questions on the Green Day albums and that specific era. In between the multiple-choice questions you will also be asked to complete the lyrics from certain Green Day albums.

There will also be sections on each of the band members in profile

Each section can be cross referenced against the answers provided towards the end of the book.

Grab a drink, a pencil, put on some Green Day and enjoy the quizbook – or take it to your friends and fill out together – quiz your best mate who claims to know everything about Green Day and see how much they truly know.

Most of all – enjoy the journey of this band from small intimate gigs to world tours.

B Demure

Green Day Quizbook

Contents

Early Days

1. What was the name of the band before they settled on Green Day?

   a) Saint Grace ☐

   b) Underkill ☐

   c) Sweet Children ☐

   d) On Saturday ☐

2. Which area of California did the band originate?

   a) Vallejo ☐

   b) Richmond ☐

   c) Albany ☐

   d) Rodeo ☐

3. How old were Armstrong and Dirnt when they first started playing music together?

   a) 12 ☐

   b) 13 ☐

   c) 15 ☐

   d) 16 ☐

4. Upon original formation of the band Mike played guitar - who was the bands original bass player?

    a) Sean Hughes ☐

    b) Steve Power ☐

    c) Sean Power ☐

    d) Steve Hughes ☐

5. Who was the bands original drummer when Armstrong and Dirnt first formed the band?

    a) Raj Bhatia ☐

    b) Ravi Punjabi ☐

    c) Ravi Bhatia ☐

    d) Raj Punjabi ☐

6. Which Tim Armstrong band did Billie Joe state was a major influence?

    a) Transplants ☐

    b) Rancid ☐

    c) Operation Ivy ☐

    d) Downfall ☐

7. Where did the band's first live performance take place in October 1987?

   a) Rod's Hickory Pit ☐

   b) Music Box ☐

   c) Troubadour ☐

   d) The Echo ☐

8. Which drummer was replaced by Tré? He had been the bands drummer since 1988

   a) John Hastings ☐

   b) Ian Kiffmeyer ☐

   c) Ian Hastings ☐

   d) John Kiffmeyer ☐

9. Which band did Tré leave to join Green Day?

   a) The Charge ☐

   b) The Lookouts ☐

   c) Pure Density ☐

   d) Outlive ☐

10. What was the name of the band's debut E.P released in April 1989?

a) 1,000 hours ☐

b) 10 Minutes ☐

c) 60 Seconds ☐

d) 7 Days ☐

(ANSWERS CAN BE FOUND ON PAGE 84)

SECTION TWO

39/Smooth 1990

1. Which independent record label released the album?
    a. Brainfeeder Records ☐

    b. Lookout! Records ☐

    c. Stones Throw Records ☐

    d. Archive Records ☐

2. In which studio was the album recorded?
    a. Hyde Steet, San Diego ☐

    b. Light Hail, San Diego ☐

    c. Different Fur, San Francisco ☐

    d. Art of Ears, San Francisco ☐

3. Which music venue did Green Day regularly perform at during this era?
    a. 924 Gilman Street ☐

    b. Ashkenaz Music Center ☐

    c. The Back Room ☐

    d. Under the Arch Bar ☐

4. The album was recorded around Christmas 1989 for what reason?

    a. They had time off from school ☐

    b. They used their Christmas money ☐

    c. Mike worked at the studio part time ☐

    d. It was the cheapest time of year ☐

5. What is the title of the opening track on the album?

    a. At the Library with Waba Sé Wasca ☐

    b. Going to Pasalacqua ☐

    c. Road to Acceptance ☐

    d. Rest ☐

6. What is the setting of the black and white image on the albums front cover?

    a. An Industrial Site ☐

    b. A Railway Track ☐

    c. A Cemetery ☐

    d. A Beachfront ☐

7. Who designed the cover of the album?

    a. Stephen Michaels ☐

    b. Jesse Michaels ☐

    c. Jesse Wright ☐

    d. Stephen Wright ☐

8. Complete the title of the final track from the album "The Judge's _____"

    a. Brother ☐

    b. Dictate ☐

    c. Decision ☐

    d. Daughter ☐

9. What sound can be heard at the start of album track "Green Day"?

    a. A Bong Bubbling ☐

    b. A Police Siren ☐

    c. A Spray Can ☐

    d. A Gunshot ☐

10. What is the title of the E.P that the band also released in 1990?

    a. Blabby ☐

    b. Blobby ☐

    c. Slappy ☐

    d. Sloppy ☐

(ANSWERS CAN BE FOUND ON PAGE 85)

Kerplunk 1991

1. What is the opening track on Kerplunk?

    a) 2000 Light Years Away ☐

    b) Private Ale ☐

    c) Christie Rd ☐

    d) Android ☐

2. How many copies did the album sell on the first day of its release?

    a) 100 ☐

    b) 1,000 ☐

    c) 5,000 ☐

    d) 10,000 ☐

3. The front cover of the album is a drawing of a girl holding a gun - but what can be seen on her t-shirt?

    a) A Flower ☐

    b) A Rainbow ☐

    c) A Skull ☐

    d) A Heart ☐

4. Which album track is written and performed by Tré?

    a) Android ☐

    b) 80 ☐

    c) Dominated Love Slave ☐

    d) No One Knows ☐

5. Complete this album track title "One for the _____"

    a) Quarterbacks ☐

    b) Razorbacks ☐

    c) Century ☐

    d) Decade ☐

6. In which European City did the band start their debut European tour?

    a) Dublin ☐

    b) Riga ☐

    c) Milan ☐

    d) Barcelona ☐

7. In December 1991 the band performed in which English City? It would become a record release party after they had received a number of copies of Kerplunk in advance of its formal release

    a) Manchester ☐

    b) London ☐

    c) Southampton ☐

    d) Leicester ☐

8. Which album track was re-recorded and included on the Dookie album?

    a) Chump ☐

    b) Pulling Teeth ☐

    c) Basket Case ☐

    d) Welcome to Paradise ☐

9. What is the title of the final track on the album?

    a) Who Wrote Holden Caulfield ☐

    b) Words I Might Have Ate ☐

    c) One of My Lies ☐

    d) A Change is Coming ☐

10. In 1990 the band released an E.P entitled "Sweet Children" which song by The Who is covered on the record?

    a) My Generation ☐

    b) Behind Blue Eyes ☐

    c) Pinball Wizard ☐

    d) I Can't Explain ☐

(ANSWERS CAN BE FOUND ON PAGE 86)

Billie Joe in profile

1. In what year was Billie Joe born?

   a) 1969 ☐

   b) 1970 ☐

   c) 1971 ☐

   d) 1972 ☐

2. What is the name of Billie Joes wife who he married in 1994?

   a) Adrienne ☐

   b) Anastasia ☐

   c) Annie ☐

   d) Arlene ☐

3. How many children does Armstrong have?

   a) One ☐

   b) Two ☐

   c) Three ☐

   d) Four ☐

4. What record label did Billie Joe co-found in 1997?

   a) BJA Records ☐

   b) CALA Records ☐

   c) Adeline Records ☐

   d) Armstrong Records ☐

5. What high school did he attend?

   a) John Swett ☐

   b) Pinole Valley ☐

   c) De Anza ☐

   d) Richmond ☐

6. Oakland Coffee Works was co-founded by Billie Joe in 2015 - what is it called now?

   a) Punk Bunny Coffee ☐

   b) Punk Fish Coffee ☐

   c) Coffee Rocks ☐

   d) Coffee Punk Rock ☐

7. How many siblings does Armstrong have?

    a) None ☐

    b) Two ☐

    c) Five ☐

    d) Six ☐

8. Who did Armstrong collaborate with on the 2015 album 'Foreverly'?

    a) Norah Jones ☐

    b) Lady Gaga ☐

    c) Adele ☐

    d) Taylor Swift ☐

9. What is the name of the cover's album Billie Joe released in 2020?

    a) No Fun Mondays ☐

    b) Only on Sunday ☐

    c) Could be Tuesday ☐

    d) Why Wait for Friday ☐

10. What is the name of the band that Billie Joe performs with alongside Aaron Cometbus?

    a) Changing Muskets ☐

    b) Reload and Fire ☐

    c) Pinhead Gunpowder ☐

    d) Insane Pushead ☐

(ANSWERS CAN BE FOUND ON PAGE 87)

SECTION FIVE

Dookie 1994

1. Prior to the release of Dookie which record label did the band sign a five-album deal with?

    a) Reload ☐

    b) Reprise ☐

    c) Repeat ☐

    d) Repair ☐

2. How long did the album take to record?

    a) Three Days ☐

    b) Three Weeks ☐

    c) Three Months ☐

    d) Six Months ☐

3. At which festival did the band start an infamous mud fight?

    a) Rock AM Ring ☐

    b) Reading ☐

    c) Woodstock '94 ☐

    d) Glastonbury ☐

4. Which track from Dookie was the first single the band released?

    a) Basket Case ☐

    b) Welcome to Paradise ☐

    c) When I Come Around ☐

    d) Longview ☐

5. What is the title of the hidden track on the album? Performed by Tré

    a) All by Myself ☐

    b) I'm All Alone ☐

    c) Only Me ☐

    d) Me, Myself and My Mind's Eye ☐

6. What is the setting for the music video for "Basket Case"?

    a) A Police Station ☐

    b) A Shipyard ☐

    c) A Mental Institution ☐

    d) A High School ☐

7. Who produced the album alongside the band?

   a) Mike Graham ☐

   b) Rob Graham ☐

   c) Mike Cavallo ☐

   d) Rob Cavallo ☐

8. Complete this song title from the album "Having a _____"

   a) Dream ☐

   b) Blast ☐

   c) Party ☐

   d) Beer ☐

9. What would best describe the front cover of the album?

   a) Bombs Being Dropped ☐

   b) A Crowd of People ☐

   c) A Graffiti Artist working ☐

   d) A Party Scene ☐

10. How many copies of Dookie were sold worldwide?

a) 3 million ☐

b) 5 million ☐

c) 10 million ☐

d) 20 million ☐

(ANSWERS CAN BE FOUND ON PAGE 88)

SECTION SIX

Complete the Dookie Lyrics....

1. I'm not growing up; I'm just burning out and I stepped in line to walk amongst the _____

2. Takin' all you down with me, explosives duct-taped to my _____

3. Strange how you've become my biggest _____ and I've never even seen your face

4. I'm feeling like a dog in heat, barred indoors from the _____ street

5. Pay attention to the _____ streets and the broken homes

6. Is she ultra-violent? Is she _____?

7. I am one of those melodramatic _____

8. Scream at me until my _____ bleed

9. I'm just a _____, wasting your time

10. I'm a loser and a user, so I don't need no
    _____

11. _____ and strung out on
    confusion

12. And now I think I'm sick and I wanna go
    _____

13. Will you pop up again and be my
    _____ friend

14. Let's _____ the bridge we torched two
    thousand times before

15. I went to your _____ but no-one was
    there

(ANSWERS CAN BE FOUND ON PAGE 89)

Insomniac 1995

1. What was the first single to be released from Insomniac?

    a) Stuart and the Ave ☐

    b) 86 ☐

    c) Geek Stink Breath ☐

    d) Stuck With Me ☐

2. What name was considered for the album before settling on Insomniac?

    a) Jesus Christ Supermarket ☐

    b) Jesus in a Traffic Jam ☐

    c) Jesus at the Drive Thru ☐

    d) Jesus Speaks, We Repeat ☐

3. The album cover is a collage entitled "God Told Me to Skin You Alive" and was created by which artist?

    a) William De Koht ☐

    b) Winston De Koht ☐

    c) William Smith ☐

    d) Winston Smith ☐

4. What is the opening track of the album?

    a) Brat ☐

    b) Armatage Shanks ☐

    c) No Pride ☐

    d) Bab's Uvula Who? ☐

5. The album peaked at number one in which European country's Official album chart?

    a) Iceland ☐

    b) Finland ☐

    c) Germany ☐

    d) Italy ☐

6. Album track "Westbound Sign" features in which 2006 Disney/Pixar film?

   a) The Incredibles ☐

   b) Finding Nemo ☐

   c) Ratatouille ☐

   d) Cars ☐

7. Alongside Brain Stew which other song from the album was released as a joint single?

   a) Panic Song ☐

   b) 86 ☐

   c) Jaded ☐

   d) Tight Wad Hill ☐

8. What is the final track on the album?

   a) Walking Contradiction ☐

   b) Westbound Sign ☐

   c) No Pride ☐

   d) Armatage Shanks ☐

9. Shortly after releasing this album the band released a live EP in South America, Australia and Eurasia - what was its title?

    a) At the Parking Lot ☐

    b) Bowling Bowling Bowling Parking Parking ☐

    c) You, I, Me and Us ☐

    d) Love, Lost, Lose, Lover ☐

10. Which Operation Ivy song was covered and released on the EP?

    a) Strength ☐

    b) Grace ☐

    c) Knowledge ☐

    d) Power ☐

(ANSWERS CAN BE FOUND ON PAGE 90)

SECTION EIGHT

Nimrod 1997

1. What best describes the front cover of the Nimrod album?

    a) Nimrod covering two faces ☐

    b) Nimrod covering naked ladies ☐

    c) Nimrod in spray paint ☐

    d) Nimrod across famous artwork ☐

2. What number did the album peak at in the US Billboard 200 chart?

    a) 2 ☐

    b) 5 ☐

    c) 10 ☐

    d) 40 ☐

3. Which additional instrument does Billie Joe play on "Walking Alone"?

    a) Harmonica ☐

    b) 12-string guitar ☐

    c) Violin ☐

    d) Trumpet ☐

4. What is the opening track of the album?

   a) All the Time ☐

   b) Worry Rock ☐

   c) Hitchin' a Ride ☐

   d) Nice Guys Finish Last ☐

5. Which album track is an instrumental?

   a) Scattered ☐

   b) Last Ride In ☐

   c) Uptight ☐

   d) Jinx ☐

6. The band recorded the album in Los Angeles and stayed at the Sunset Marquis Hotel - during their stay what did Tré throw out of his hotel room window?

   a) A Television ☐

   b) His Drums ☐

   c) Mikes Bass ☐

   d) His Alarm Clock ☐

7. How many tracks are there on the standard edition of the album?

    a) 10 ☐

    b) 15 ☐

    c) 18 ☐

    d) 22 ☐

8. Petra Haden features on the album - what instrument does she play on "Hitchin' a ride" and "Last Ride In"?

    a) Violin ☐

    b) Banjo ☐

    c) Harp ☐

    d) Clarinet ☐

9. Complete the title of this album track "_____ For a Day"

    a) Alive ☐

    b) Dead ☐

    c) Woman ☐

    d) King ☐

10. Which award did the band win for "Good Riddance (Time of Your Life)" at the 1998 VMAs?

a) Best Live Performance ☐

b) Best Alternative Video ☐

c) Best Band Video ☐

d) Best Song ☐

(ANSWERS CAN BE FOUND ON PAGE 91)

Mike in Profile

1. What is Mike's full birth name?

    a) Michael Ryan Walker ☐

    b) Michael Peter Walker ☐

    c) Michael Peter Pritchard ☐

    d) Michael Ryan Pritchard ☐

2. At which festival did Mike lose one of his teeth? After being tackled by a member of the security staff who mistook him for a fan

    a) Download ☐

    b) Reading ☐

    c) Woodstock '94 ☐

    d) Glastonbury ☐

3. Which band did Mike play bass and provide backing vocals on their 1994 album "How to Make Enemies and Irritate People"?

   a) Riverdales ☐

   b) Screeching Weasel ☐

   c) The Methadones ☐

   d) Sludgeworth ☐

4. What is the date of Mike's birthday? Also known as Star Wars Day

   a) May 4th ☐

   b) July 12th ☐

   c) March 18th ☐

   d) January 1st ☐

5. Which other band has Mike been part of since 1999?

   a) The Fantasists ☐

   b) The Destructors ☐

   c) The Detonators ☐

   d) The Frustrators ☐

6. After which song by The Clash is his diner named after?

    a) White Riot ☐

    b) Rudie Can't Fail ☐

    c) Bankrobber ☐

    d) Guns of Brixton ☐

7. How many times has Mike been married?

    a) Once ☐

    b) Twice ☐

    c) Three Times ☐

    d) Four Times ☐

8. How old was Mike when he first met Billie Joe?

    a) Ten ☐

    b) Six ☐

    c) Fourteen ☐

    d) Eleven ☐

9. What is Mikes signature bass guitar that he has used since 1997?

    a) Fender Mustang ☐

    b) Squier Mustang ☐

    c) Ibanez MD85 ☐

    d) Fender Precision ☐

10. As a child what did Mike want to be when he grew up? It was revealed by Billie Joe in a 2021 interview

    a) A Photographer ☐

    b) A Chef ☐

    c) A Comedian ☐

    d) A Fireman ☐

(ANSWERS CAN BE FOUND ON PAGE 92)

Warning 2000

1. In 1999 prior to the release of Warning who joined the band as a touring guitarist and remains to this day?

    a) Mark Black ☐

    b) Jason White ☐

    c) Jason Black ☐

    d) Mark White ☐

2. At the 2001 California Music Awards how many awards did the band win? They won every category they had been nominated

    a) Five ☐

    b) Six ☐

    c) Eight ☐

    d) Eleven ☐

3. In 2002 who did Green Day co-headline with on the Pop Disaster Tour?

   a) Blink-182 ☐

   b) Sum 41 ☐

   c) Bowling for Soup ☐

   d) Jimmy Eat World ☐

4. Released in August 2020 - what is the title of the lead single from the album?

   a) Misery ☐

   b) Castaway ☐

   c) Hold On ☐

   d) Minority ☐

5. Complete the title of this album track "Deadbeat _____"

   a) Holiday ☐

   b) Disaster ☐

   c) Fantasy ☐

   d) Lifestyle ☐

6. What additional instrument does Tré play on the album?

    a) Mandolin ☐

    b) Ukelele ☐

    c) Accordion ☐

    d) Harmonica ☐

7. What type of organ does Mike play on "Misery"?

    a) VOX ☐

    b) Farfisa ☐

    c) Church ☐

    d) Fairground ☐

8. The second single from the album was title track "Warning" - in the music video what does the protagonist rub into his eyes? He also swallows toothpaste and crosses a police cordon

    a) A lemon ☐

    b) Chocolate ☐

    c) Paint ☐

    d) Soap ☐

9. Which file sharing website was the album leaked onto three weeks before it was released?

    a) Napster ☐

    b) Limewire ☐

    c) Morpheus ☐

    d) WinMX ☐

10. "Waiting" was the final single to be released from the album - which 1964 Petula Clark song is the riff based on?

    a) This is My Song ☐

    b) The Song of My Life ☐

    c) Kiss Me Goodbye ☐

    d) Downtown ☐

(ANSWERS CAN BE FOUND ON PAGE 93)

SECTION ELEVEN

Complete the Nimrod and Warning Lyrics

Complete the lyrics from Nimrod and Warning (Five from each album)

1. Don't pat yourself on the back, you might break your _____

2. There's a _____ at the fountain of youth

3. I woke up on the wrong side of the _____

4. Sometimes, I need to _____. Sometimes, I need to admit that I ain't right

5. _____ of memories and dead skin on trial

6. Better _____ and safety-sealed communities

7. The catastrophic hymns from yesterday of _____

8. Downtown, lights will be shining on me like a new _____ ring

9. I pledge allegiance to the _____

10. Red light special at the _____

(ANSWERS CAN BE FOUND ON PAGE 94)

SECTION TWELVE

American Idiot 2004

1. What was the name of the album that should have been released in Summer 2003? However, with the album almost finished the master tapes were mysteriously stolen - the band started recording from scratch and hence American Idiot was borne

   a) Beer and Loneliness ☐

   b) Cigars and Champagne Bars ☐

   c) Cigarettes and Valentines ☐

   d) Whiskey and the Heartland ☐

2. What was the name of the live CD and DVD released as part of the American Idiot tour? Recorded at Milton Keynes National Bowl, England

   a) Pages of a Bible ☐

   b) Pages of a Book ☐

   c) Bullet in a Bible ☐

   d) Bullet in a Book ☐

3. Which author wrote "Green Day: American Idiots & The New Punk Explosion" in 2006?

   a) Ben Myers ☐

   b) Chris Myers ☐

   c) Ben Stark ☐

   d) Chris Stark ☐

4. What heart shaped object features on the front cover of the album?

   a) Necklace ☐

   b) Flower ☐

   c) Box ☐

   d) Grenade ☐

5. How many singles were released from the album?

   a) Two ☐

   b) Three ☐

   c) Five ☐

   d) Six ☐

6. Complete the title of this album track - "Give Me _____"

    a) Loneliness ☐

    b) Everything ☐

    c) Satisfaction ☐

    d) Novacaine ☐

7. What is the longest track on the album? Running at 9 minutes 18 seconds

    a) Letterbomb ☐

    b) She's a Rebel ☐

    c) Homecoming ☐

    d) Jesus of Suburbia ☐

8. What song on the album finishes with the line "And Don't Wear It Out!"

    a) Are We the Waiting ☐

    b) American Idiot ☐

    c) Extraordinary Girl ☐

    d) St. Jimmy ☐

9. Which feminist punk pioneer provided guest vocals on album track "Letterbomb"?

   a) Kathleen Hanna ☐

   b) Charlene Hanna ☐

   c) Kathleen Brown ☐

   d) Charlene Brown ☐

10. What is the title of the final track of the album?

   a) Whatsername ☐

   b) Wake Me Up When September Ends ☐

   c) Holiday ☐

   d) Homecoming ☐

(ANSWERS CAN BE FOUND ON PAGE 95)

21st Century Breakdown 2009

1. Which supermarket chain refused to stock the album as it contained a Parental Advisory sticker?

    a) Costco ☐

    b) Wal-Mart ☐

    c) Target ☐

    d) Kroger ☐

2. Who produced the album alongside the band?

    a) Butch Vig ☐

    b) Rick Rubin ☐

    c) Brian Eno ☐

    d) Tony Visconti ☐

3. What is the title of the opening track? A 57 second introduction to the album

    a) Start of the Century ☐

    b) Song of the Century ☐

    c) Song of the Celebration ☐

    d) Start of the Celebration ☐

4. What was the first single to be released from
    the album in April 2009?

    a) 21 Guns ☐

    b) 21ˢᵗ Century Breakdown ☐

    c) Last of the American Girls ☐

    d) Know Your Enemy ☐

5. Which musician is credited as a songwriter on
    "21 Guns" to avoid a potential plagiarism
    lawsuit due to the chorus being very similar to
    Mott the Hoople hit "All the Young Dudes"?

    a) Marc Bolan ☐

    b) Elton John ☐

    c) Freddie Mercury ☐

    d) David Bowie ☐

6. Which 1966 song by The Who was recorded
    and released as a bonus track on the deluxe
    edition of the album?

    a) Boris the Spider ☐

    b) A Legal Matter ☐

    c) A Quick One, While He's Away ☐

    d) I'm a Boy ☐

7. The album continues the rock opera style of American Idiot divided into three individual acts - which of the below is NOT the name of one of the acts on the album?

    a) Magicians and Mermaids ☐

    b) Charlatans and Saints ☐

    c) Heroes and Cons ☐

    d) Horseshoes and Handgrenades ☐

8. Complete the title of this album track – "Before the _____"

    a) Lobotomy ☐

    b) Collapse ☐

    c) Ending ☐

    d) Beginning ☐

9. What are the names of the two main protagonists of the 21st Century Breakdown album?

    a) Carol and Chris ☐

    b) Adam and Eve ☐

    c) Christian and Gloria ☐

    d) Nero and Cleo ☐

10. Album track "American Eulogy" is split into two sections - the second part features lead vocals by Mike - what is it entitled?

a) In the Past ☐

b) Modern World ☐

c) Forgotten World ☐

d) Now is the Future ☐

(ANSWERS CAN BE FOUND ON PAGE 96)

Complete the American Idiot & 21ˢᵗ Century Breakdown Lyrics

Complete the lyrics from American Idiot and 21st Century Breakdown (Five from each)

1. Now everybody do the propaganda and sing along to the age of _____

2. Get my television fix, sitting on my _____

3. I beg to dream and differ from the hollow lies, this is the _____ of the rest of our lives

4. My _____ hearts the only thing that's beating

5. Ring out the bells again, like we did when _____ began

6. My generation is zero, I never made it as a _____ class hero

7. The insurgency will rise, when the bloods been _____

8. Dying, everyone's reminding hearts are washed in _____

9. Oh, bless me lord for I have sinned, it's been a lifetime since I last _____

10. She wears her overcoat for the coming of the _____ winter

(ANSWERS CAN BE FOUND ON PAGE 97)

UNO!, DOS!, TRE! (Three Albums) 2012

1. Which regular touring guitarist joined the band to help with recording the album? (He also worked on the following two albums)

   a) Brandon O'Sullivan ☐

   b) Jason White ☐

   c) Brandon White ☐

   d) Jason O'Sullivan ☐

2. At which 2012 music festival did Dirnt and Armstrong smash their instruments after Billie Joe was angered by their set being cut short?

   a) Bumbershoot ☐

   b) Sasquatch! ☐

   c) Lollapalooza ☐

   d) iHeartRadio ☐

3. Released in July 2012 what was the first single to be released from "¡Uno!"?

   a) Kill the DJ ☐

   b) Oh Love ☐

   c) Let Yourself Go ☐

   d) Fell for You ☐

4. On track "Loss of Control" from "¡Uno!" the band sampled "Pack It Up" originally recorded by which band?

   a) The Clash ☐

   b) The Cardigans ☐

   c) The Police ☐

   d) The Pretenders ☐

5. The album "¡Dos!" is said to be the bands take on which musical genre?

   a) Garage Rock ☐

   b) Lounge Rock ☐

   c) Classic Rock ☐

   d) Glam Rock ☐

6. What was the only single released from ¡Dos! In October 2012?

    a) Wild One ☐

    b) Lazy Bones ☐

    c) Lady Cobra ☐

    d) Stray Heart ☐

7. The final track on "¡Dos!" is a ballad written in tribute to which singer?

    a) Karen Carpenter ☐

    b) Amy Winehouse ☐

    c) Ella Fitzgerald ☐

    d) Whitney Houston ☐

8. "The Forgotten" features on the soundtrack of which film?

    a) The Twilight Saga: Breaking Dawn - Part 2 ☐

    b) Resident Evil: Damnation ☐

    c) Smiley ☐

    d) The Possession ☐

9. What is the title of the single released from
   ¡Tré!?

   a) 99 Revolutions ☐

   b) Amanda ☐

   c) X-Kid ☐

   d) Missing You ☐

10. The opening album track on "¡Tré!" - "Brutal
    Love" uses the melody from which Sam
    Cooke song?

    a) A Change is Gonna Come ☐

    b) Bring It on Home to Me ☐

    c) Wonderful World ☐

    d) Cupid ☐

(ANSWERS CAN BE FOUND ON PAGE 98)

Revolution Radio 2016

1. What was the first single to be released from the album?

    a) Bang Bang ☐

    b) Revolution Radio ☐

    c) Still Breathing ☐

    d) Youngblood ☐

2. What best describes the front cover of the album?

    a) A Radio on Fire ☐

    b) A Flag on Fire ☐

    c) A Tank exploded ☐

    d) A WWII wireless ☐

3. What is the opening track of the album?

    a) Say Goodbye ☐

    b) Troubled Times ☐

    c) Somewhere Now ☐

    d) Outlaws ☐

4. Complete the title of this album track "Too _____ to Die"

   a) Cute ☐

   b) Stupid ☐

   c) Young ☐

   d) Dumb ☐

5. Which album track shares its title with a film that featured Billie Joe released in 2016?

   a) Bouncing off the Wall ☐

   b) Still Breathing ☐

   c) Bang Bang ☐

   d) Ordinary World ☐

6. "Still Breathing" attributes writing credits to the writers of which 2013 The Struts song due to similarities between the songs Melodie's?

   a) A Change has Come ☐

   b) Could Have Been Me ☐

   c) If Only ☐

   d) Talk to Me ☐

7. Which song from the album is split into three parts?

    a) Forever Now □

    b) Forever Again □

    c) Never Now □

    d) Never Again □

8. Who provides trumpet on track "Bouncing Off the Wall"? He had also featured on the American Idiot tour

    a) Richard Blake □

    b) Ronnie Haynes □

    c) Ronnie Blake □

    d) Richard Haynes □

9. What number did the album peak at in the UK and US album charts?

    a) 1 □

    b) 5 □

    c) 10 □

    d) 20 □

10. What is the name of the greatest hits album the band released in 2017?

   a) God Wishes He Was Us ☐

   b) In God We Rock ☐

   c) God Loves Us ☐

   d) Gods Favorite Band ☐

(ANSWERS CAN BE FOUND ON PAGE 99)

SECTION SEVENTEEN

Father of All... 2020

1. What was the name of the tour the band went on with Fall Out Boy and Weezer?
   a) Pioneers of Punk Tour ☐
   b) Punk Party Tour ☐
   c) Hella Mega Tour ☐
   d) Hell Yeah for Us Tour ☐

2. Opening track and lead single "Father of All..." features a riff from which Jimi Hendrix Experience song?
   a) Hey Joe ☐
   b) Fire ☐
   c) Purple Haze ☐
   d) Voodoo Child ☐

3. The music video for "Father of All" pay homage to which music legend?

   a) Elton John ☐

   b) Kurt Cobain ☐

   c) Elvis Presley ☐

   d) John Lennon ☐

4. Which sports league did Green Day sign a two-year agreement with in 2019?

   a) National Football League ☐

   b) National Hockey League ☐

   c) National Basketball Association ☐

   d) Major League Baseball ☐

5. On the front cover of the standard album which mythical creature partial covers the explicit word that completes the album title?

   a) A Unicorn ☐

   b) A Dragon ☐

   c) A Griffin ☐

   d) Bigfoot ☐

6. The album is Green Day's shortest studio album to date - what is the total runtime?

    a) 18:37 ☐

    b) 26:12 ☐

    c) 21:21 ☐

    d) 34:59 ☐

7. Oh Yeah! Features a sample of which singers' version of "Do You Wanna Touch Me?"

    a) Suzi Quatro ☐

    b) PJ Harvey ☐

    c) Alanis Morissette ☐

    d) Joan Jett ☐

8. Oh Yeah! Became the official theme song to which 2020 WWE PPV event?

    a) Payback ☐

    b) Backlash ☐

    c) Summerslam ☐

    d) Wrestlemania ☐

9. Complete the title of this album track "Take the Money and _____ "

    a) Crawl ☐

    b) Run ☐

    c) Jog ☐

    d) Walk ☐

10. What number did the album peak at in the UK album charts?

    a) 1 ☐

    b) 5 ☐

    c) 10 ☐

    d) 25 ☐

(ANSWERS CAN BE FOUND ON PAGE 100)

Saviors 2024

1. Who produced the Saviors album?

   a) Butch Vig ☐

   b) Tim Armstrong ☐

   c) Rob Cavallo ☐

   d) Brian Eno ☐

2. The cover of the album features a photograph from 1978 during riots in which country?

   a) Brazil ☐

   b) South Africa ☐

   c) Venezuela ☐

   d) Northern Ireland ☐

3. What was the albums lead single and opening track of the album?

   a) The American Dream is Killing Me ☐

   b) Dilemma ☐

   c) Bobby Sox ☐

   d) Living in the '20s ☐

4. Complete the title of this album track "Look Ma, No _____"

   a) Hands ☐

   b) Brains ☐

   c) Drama ☐

   d) Problem ☐

5. Which album track is due to be on the soundtrack of the NHL 25 video game?

   a) 1981 ☐

   b) Corvette Girl ☐

   c) Coma City ☐

   d) One Eyed Bastard ☐

6. Prior to the release of Saviors the band recorded a BBC live session and released it as an album - in what London studio was it recorded?

   a) Maida Vale Studios ☐

   b) Abbey Road Studios ☐

   c) White City Studios ☐

   d) Leicester Square Studios ☐

7. Early reports suggested that the title of the album would be named after what year?

    a) 1822 ☐

    b) 1969 ☐

    c) 1972 ☐

    d) 1999 ☐

8. Which of these bands supported Green Day on the European leg of the Saviors tour?

    a) The Libertines ☐

    b) The Arctic Monkeys ☐

    c) The Vines ☐

    d) The Hives ☐

9. At what festival did the band first debut a song from The Saviors album in October 2023?

    a) Best Friends Forever ☐

    b) Sema Fest ☐

    c) Life is Beautiful ☐

    d) When We Were Young ☐

10. In January 2024 the band played a surprise performance at Rockefeller Center Station - who joined them playing tambourine?

    a) Jimmy Kimmel ☐

    b) Jimmy Fallon ☐

    c) Jimmy Page ☐

    d) Jimmy Carr ☐

(ANSWERS CAN BE FOUND ON PAGE 101)

Tre in profile

1. In which European country was Tré born?

    a) Belgium ☐

    b) Germany ☐

    c) England ☐

    d) France ☐

2. What is Tré's birth name?

    a) Frank Edwin Wright III ☐

    b) Terence Culheart ☐

    c) Frank Edwards ☐

    d) Francis de Marquand ☐

3. What area of California did Tré grow up in?

    a) Willits ☐

    b) Irvine ☐

    c) Long Beach ☐

    d) Malibu ☐

4. What magazine named Tré as 'Best Punk Drummer" in 2011?

   a) Modern Drummer ☐

   b) Rhythm ☐

   c) DRUM! ☐

   d) DownBeat ☐

5. How many children does Tré have?

   a) One ☐

   b) Two ☐

   c) Three ☐

   d) Four ☐

6. Which Beatles song did Tré perform alongside Ringo Starr at the Rock and Roll Hall of Fame ceremony?

   a) I Feel Fine ☐

   b) Boys ☐

   c) Now and Then ☐

   d) Oh! Darling ☐

7. How many times has Tré been married?

   a) Never ☐

   b) One ☐

   c) Three ☐

   d) Five ☐

8. What age did Tre turn just two days after the release of album ¡Tré!?

   a) 45 ☐

   b) 30 ☐

   c) 40 ☐

   d) 35 ☐

9. Which Bob Dylan album does Tré state is his favourite album of all time?

   a) Slow Train Coming ☐

   b) Desire ☐

   c) Blonde on Blonde ☐

   d) Blood on the Tracks ☐

10. In 2020 which country legend did Cool drum for after the death of his drummer Paul English?

a) Garth Brooks ☐

b) Neil Young ☐

c) Merle Haggard ☐

d) Willie Nelson ☐

(ANSWERS CAN BE FOUND ON PAGE 102)

SECTION TWENTY

Spinoffs, Side Projects and Covers

1. The band recorded an album for Tim Armstrong's record label Adeline Records and released it secretly under which band name?

    a) The Wireless ☐

    b) The Radio ☐

    c) The Network ☐

    d) The Television ☐

2. What is Mikes alternative name in this band?

    a) Peter Mondri-ain't ☐

    b) John Vermeer ☐

    c) Van Gough ☐

    d) Rembraandt ☐

3. What was the name of the album released?

    a) Little Little 2020 ☐

    b) Change Change 2020 ☐

    c) Money Money 2020 ☐

    d) Shock Shock 2020 ☐

4. Green Day recorded a cover of which song by The Clash in 2004?

    a) I Fought the Law ☐

    b) Train in Vain ☐

    c) Rock the Casbah ☐

    d) I Fought the Law ☐

5. Formed in 2007 what is the name of the Garage Rock Green Day side project?

    a) Middlesboro Hot Tubs ☐

    b) Middlesboro Time Machine ☐

    c) Foxboro Hot Tubs ☐

    d) Foxboro Time Machine ☐

6. In 2008 the band released a garage rock inspired album under the name Foxboro Hot Tubs - what was the album's title?

    a) Stop Drop and Roll!!! ☐

    b) Ready Aim and Fire!!! ☐

    c) Hold, Hold Release? ☐

    d) Mirror, Signal, Drive ☐

7. Which of the Green Day albums was made into a rock musical in 2009?

    a) Insomniac ☐

    b) American Idiot ☐

    c) Dookie ☐

    d) 21st Century Breakdown ☐

8. In 2014 the band released a compilation album of demos from ¡Uno! ¡Dos! and ¡Tré! - what was it titled?

    a) Demolicious ☐

    b) Demolition ☐

    c) Demonstration ☐

    d) DemonDayz ☐

9. In May 2020 the band released a cover of which Blondie song?

    a) Atomic ☐

    b) The Tide is High ☐

    c) Dreaming ☐

    d) Denis ☐

10. In 2021 which Kiss song did the band cover and release as a live single?

    a) Lick It Up ☐

    b) Detroit Rock City ☐

    c) I Was Made for Lovin' You ☐

    d) Rock and Roll All Nite ☐

(ANSWERS CAN BE FOUND ON PAGE 103)

Opening Lyrics Quiz

Name the Green Day song from the opening lyric provided... (Album that the track features on provided in brackets)

1. (Nimrod) I was a young boy that had big plans

   _____

2. (Nimrod) Another turning point, a fork stuck in the road

   _____

3. (American Idiot) I am the son of rage and love

   _____

4. (Kerplunk) I sit alone in my bedroom, staring at the Walls

   _____

5. (Dookie) I don't know you, but I think I hate
    you

    _____

6. (Dookie) I heard you crying loud, all the way
    across town

    _____

7. (Insomniac) I'm having trouble trying to sleep,
    I'm counting sheep but running out

    _____

8. (American Idiot) Hear the sound of the falling
    rain, coming down like an Armageddon flame

    _____

9. (21st Century Breakdown) She puts her
    makeup on, like graffiti on the walls of the
    heartland

    _____

10. (¡Tre!) Hey, little kid, did you wake up late
    one day and you're not so young, but you're
    still dumb

    _____

ANSWERS

Section One: Early Days

1. c) Sweet Children ☐

2. d) Rodeo ☐

3. c) 15 ☐

4. a) Sean Hughes ☐

5. d) Raj Punjabi ☐

6. c) Operation Ivy ☐

7. a) Rod's Hickory Pit ☐

8. d) John Kiffmeyer ☐

9. b) The Lookouts ☐

10 a) 1,000 hours ☐

/10

Section Two: 39/Smooth 1990

1. b. Lookout! Records ☐

2. d. Art of Ears, San Francisco ☐

3. a. 924 Gilman Street ☐

4. d. It was inexpensive ☐

5. a. At the Library with Waba Sé Wasca ☐

6. c. Cemetery ☐

7. b. Jesse Michaels ☐

8. d. Daughter ☐

9. a. A Bong Bubbling ☐

10 c. Slappy ☐

/10

Section Three: Kerplunk 1991

1. a) 2000 Light Years Away ☐
2. d) 10,000 ☐
3. a) A flower ☐
4. c) Dominated Love Slave ☐
5. b) Razorbacks ☐
6. d) Barcelona ☐
7. c) Southampton ☐
8. d) Welcome to Paradise ☐
9. b) Words I Might Have Ate ☐
10 a) My Generation ☐

/10

Section Four: Billie Joe in profile

1.   d)   1972 ☐
2.   a)   Adrienne ☐
3.   b)   Two ☐
4.   c)   Adeline Records ☐
5.   b)   Pinole Valley ☐
6.   a)   Punk Bunny Coffee ☐
7.   c)   Five ☐
8.   a)   Norah Jones ☐
9.   a)   No Fun Mondays ☐
10   c)   Pinhead Gunpowder ☐

/10

Section Five: Dookie 1994

1. b) Reprise ☐

2. b) Three Weeks ☐

3. c) Woodstock '94 ☐

4. d) Longview ☐

5. a) All by Myself ☐

6. c) Mental Institution ☐

7. d) Rob Cavallo ☐

8. b) Blast ☐

9. a) Bombs Being Dropped ☐

10 d) 20 million ☐

/10

Section Six: Complete the Dookie lyric

1. Dead ☐

2. Spine ☐

3. Enemy ☐

4. Summer ☐

5. Cracked ☐

6. Disturbed ☐

7. Fools ☐

8. Ears ☐

9. Parasite ☐

10. Accuser ☐

11. Seventeen ☐

12. Home ☐

13. Special ☐

14. Nuke ☐

15. House ☐

/15

Section Seven: Insomniac 1995

1. c) Geek Stink Breath ☐

2. a) Jesus Christ Supermarket ☐

3. d) Winston Smith ☐

4. b) Armatage Shanks ☐

5. b) Finland ☐

6. d) Cars ☐

7. c) Jaded ☐

8. a) Walking Contradiction ☐

9. b) Bowling Bowling Bowling Parking Parking ☐

10 c) Knowledge ☐

/10

Section Eight: Nimrod 1997

1.   a)   Nimrod covering two faces ☐

2.   c)   10 ☐

3.   a)   Harmonica ☐

4.   d)   Nice Guys Finish Last ☐

5.   b)   Last Ride In ☐

6.   a)   A Television ☐

7.   c)   18 ☐

8.   a)   Violin ☐

9.   d)   King ☐

10   b)   Best Alternative Video ☐

/10

Section Nine: Mike in profile

1.   d)   Michael Ryan Pritchard ☐
2.   c)   Woodstock '94 ☐
3.   b)   Screeching Weasel ☐
4.   a)   May 4th ☐
5.   d)   The Frustrators ☐
6.   b)   Rudie Can't Fail ☐
7.   c)   Three ☐
8.   a)   Ten ☐
9.   d)   Fender Precision ☐
10   c)   Comedian ☐

/10

Section Ten: Warning 2000

1.   b)   Jason White ☐
2.   c)   Eight ☐
3.   a)   Blink-182 ☐
4.   d)   Minority ☐
5.   a)   Holiday ☐
6.   c)   Accordion ☐
7.   b)   Farfisa ☐
8.   d)   Soap ☐
9.   a)   Napster ☐
10   d)   Downtown ☐

/10

Section Eleven: Complete the Nimrod and Warning lyrics

1. Spine ☐

2. Drought ☐

3. Floor ☐

4. Apologize ☐

5. Tattoos ☐

6. Homes ☐

7. Misery ☐

8. Diamond ☐

9. Underworld ☐

10. Mausoleum ☐

/10

Section Twelve: American Idiot 2004

1. c) Cigarettes and Valentines ☐
2. c) Bullet in a Bible ☐
3. a) Ben Myers ☐
4. d) Grenade ☐
5. c) Five ☐
6. d) Novacaine ☐
7. c) Homecoming ☐
8. d) St. Jimmy ☐
9. a) Kathleen Hanna ☐
10 a) Whatsername ☐

/10

Section Thirteen: 21st Century Breakdown

1. b) Wal-Mart ☐

2. a) Butch Vig ☐

3. b) Song of the Century ☐

4. d) Know Your Enemy ☐

5. d) David Bowie ☐

6. c) A Quick One, While He's Away ☐

7. a) Magicians and Mermaids ☐

8. a) Lobotomy ☐

9. c) Christian and Gloria ☐

10 b) Modern World ☐

/10

Section Fourteen: Complete the American Idiot & 21st Century Breakdown Lyrics

1. Paranoia ☐

2. Crucifix ☐

3. Dawning ☐

4. Shallow ☐

5. Spring ☐

6. Working ☐

7. Sacrificed ☐

8. Misery ☐

9. Confessed ☐

10. Nuclear ☐

/10

Section Fifteen: UNO!, DOS!, TRES! 2012

1. b) Jason White ☐
2. d) iHeartRadio ☐
3. b) Oh Love ☐
4. d) The Pretenders ☐
5. a) Garage Rock ☐
6. d) Stray Heart ☐
7. b) Amy Winehouse ☐
8. a) The Twilight Saga: Breaking Dawn - Part 2 ☐
9. c) X-Kid ☐
10 b) Bring It on Home to Me ☐

/10

Section Sixteen: Revolution Radio 2016

1. a) Bang Bang ☐

2. a) A radio on fire ☐

3. c) Somewhere Now ☐

4. d) Dumb ☐

5. d) Ordinary World ☐

6. b) Could Have Been Me ☐

7. a) Forever Now ☐

8. c) Ronnie Blake ☐

9. a) 1 ☐

10 d) Gods Favorite Band ☐

/10

Section Seventeen: Father of All... 2020

1. c) Hella Mega Tour ☐
2. b) Fire ☐
3. c) Elvis Presley ☐
4. b) National Hockey League ☐
5. a) A Unicorn ☐
6. b) 26:12 ☐
7. d) Joan Jett ☐
8. b) Backlash ☐
9. a) Crawl ☐
10 a) 1 ☐

/10

Section Eighteen: Saviors 2024

1.   c)   Rob Cavallo ☐
2.   d)   Northern Ireland ☐
3.   a)   The American Dream is Killing Me ☐
4.   b)   Brains ☐
5.   d)   One Eyed Bastard ☐
6.   a)   Maida Vale Studios ☐
7.   c)   1972 ☐
8.   d)   The Hives ☐
9.   d)   When We Were Young ☐
10   b)   Jimmy Fallon ☐

/10

Section Nineteen: Tre in profile

1. b) Germany ☐
2. a) Frank Edwin Wright III ☐
3. a) Willits ☐
4. c) DRUM! ☐
5. c) Three ☐
6. b) Boys ☐
7. c) Three ☐
8. c) 40 ☐
9. d) Blood on the Tracks ☐
10 d) Willie Nelson ☐

/10

Section Twenty: Spinoffs, Side Projects and Covers

1.   c)   The Network ☐
2.   c)   Van Gough ☐
3.   c)   Money Money 2020 ☐
4.   d)   I Fought the Law ☐
5.   c)   Foxboro Hot Tubs ☐
6.   a)   Stop Drop and Roll!!! ☐
7.   b)   American Idiot ☐
8.   a)   Demolicious ☐
9.   c)   Dreaming ☐
10   d)   Rock and Roll All Nite ☐

/10

Section Twenty-One: Opening Lyrics Quiz

1. The Grouch ☐

2. Good Riddance (Time of Your Life) ☐

3. Jesus of Suburbia ☐

4. 2000 Light Years Away ☐

5. Chump ☐

6. When I Come Around ☐

7. Brain Stew ☐

8. Holiday ☐

9. Last of the American Girls ☐

10. X-Kid ☐

/10

That completes the quiz and with a total of 215 points available – where do you stand?

200-220 Punk Superstar

175-199 Totally Punk Rock

151-174 Pop Punk

101-150 Room for Improvement

51-100 Still learning the ropes.

0-50 Pop Princess

Hopefully you have enjoyed this little quiz book and it has been a challenge but your knowledge has extended and been rewarded. Now it's time to challenge your friends and family.

Take away multiple choice options for the easier questions and use the book to teach the next generation of fans about the history of this great band.

Printed in Great Britain
by Amazon

49736781R00066